THE MIDDLE AGES

JIM DANIELS

ISBN 978-0-9985140-2-4

Printed in the United States of America

RED MOUNTAIN PRESS

Santa Fe, New Mexico

for my family

1. Soccer Practice, September 11, 2001

I turned off the TV.
As coach, I studied my list of phone numbers
          but called no one.
I drove my son up the hill to Schenley Oval.
          Six kids showed, and we ran
drills, ending with a scrimmage,
          three on three, yellow pinnies
versus green—the kids demanded them.

Afterward, I clutched my equipment bag
          and carried it back to the car.
You might think I should've cancelled.
          I felt. I felt. I felt.
I just deleted the word "like" three times.

*

In our league, we didn't keep score
          though some of the kids did.
The team names were jersey colors.
          You could not cheer for your child.
Just *Go Blue!* or *Go Maroon! Go Red!*
          The kids, seven and eight, laughed
and ran in bright pinnies like cartoon birds.
          My assistant coach from Serbia
kept score. He knew no other way.

*

If the world had better things to do, no one knew
          what those things were. At least, I didn't.
I knew little about soccer: Spread out. Pass the ball.

My school president asked me to write a poem
          for him to read at homecoming
to families of dead alums. And I did. Knowing
          nothing of their grief. Spread out. Pass the ball.

*

In Doha, Qatar, teaching at our new campus,
       I took a mosque tour to learn a thing
or two. Afterward, the guide stopped me:
       So, you are from Pennsylvania.
We have heard, he said, *the U. S.*, he said,
       politely, *staged that plane crash.*
Scattered debris. We were so far apart,
       I stood sputtering in that wreckage.

       My son remembers nothing of that day.
He has been asked. They have all been asked.
       Every kid got the same trophy, no names.

The kind man had demonstrated ritual cleansing
       in the mosque washroom, the poetry
of careful words, gestures. I should have taken
       notes. I should have said/I mean/like.

He handed over my gift bag with a Koran
       and other translated Islamic texts.
I had never held a paper bag that thick, sturdy,
       as if from a store only God could shop at.
We had just eaten a traditional meal, together,
       with our hands, on the floor,
ripping meat from bone.

*

If you can tell me what I should have
       told him, where I should have
begun, I will you tell you why
       we held soccer practice
on that high hill overlooking our city.

*

Life gets away, and suddenly
       the bomb shelter you planned to build
the supplies you planned to stockpile
       the crack you planned to patch

the planned purge of your worldly possessions
  the phone call you meant to return
the insult you meant to return
  the dog you meant to love
the ant you meant to squash
  all go by the wayside
but that date on our calendars
  is forever torn out and tossed,
indecipherable instructions for grieving.

2. Giving Directions, the End of Ramadan, September 10, 2010

I often walk the trails in Schenley Park,
a two-mile loop past the dead-end turnaround
by the playground where today six cars
idled in a caravan, chugging, dismayed
the road did not continue.

*

Last summer, teaching
in the deep-sting heat of Doha,
I often passed the campus prayer rooms,
cubbyholes lined with shoes.

What can you learn in ten weeks?
Heat is one measurable thing.
Most things are not. For instance,
the heart. For instance, faith.

*

I stooped to a tinted window
and a veiled woman hesitated

before lowering it, opening
to the soft sun of September
in Pittsburgh. I wore my Pirates cap,
a member of that tribe, though they hadn't
had a winning record in 18 years.

What are you looking for? I asked.

The meadow, she said, *where is the meadow?*

I knew no place in the park
where I have walked for 24 years
called *the meadow.*
                          I directed her
to the biggest open space, which was not,
it turned out, where she wanted to be.

Did they think I lied?
That's how quick language explodes.

*

All my students, Muslim:
Qatari. Egyptian. Palestinian. Afghani.
Dressed all black or all white. Or Western.
Veiled, or not. Mascara, or not.

Thouria. Jasmine. Omar. Buthayna.
Ghamin. Jawaher. Khadra. Eman.
Shereena, Afifah. Mamoud. Aisha.

You cannot clump sand together
in that heat, that vast rainless scape.
It falls though fingers, finds its way
into everything.

*

The veiled woman led the cars in a loop
around the small intimate tree
in the circle of the turnaround
that blooms pink in spring,
rages orange in fall.

Down the trail, another car stopped me,
and another. It's Schenley *Oval*
they wanted, and I could translate the way:
loop under a highway, wind up the hill past
the closed ice rink to the soccer field.

*

In the monster mall across the street
from my apartment in Doha,
more than one of everything sprawled
across the dizzying levels—but just one
ice rink, the novelty act, on the lowest.
I looked down at laughing struggles, wild falls,
the mad splay of robes. The shock of no firm
footing, no grit—just the cold slippery surface
I grew up with.

*

I circled the trail and wound back
toward home, where more Muslims idled
on my street. *Roll down your window,*
I said, *and I will lead you there.*

They in their uniforms, me in mine.
On my street, and not. In my country,
and not. Here, where posturing Americans
wave flags and fists, while far away,
they wave flags and fists back.

*

It is easy to scoff, yet I scoff.
I who graded and ranked them,
who demanded they turn off their phones,
who did not accept late work.
Who failed them for plagiarism.

*

What happened to shame,
good old American shame? Oh,
the rotting platform, the foot
through boards, the explosion of falling.
All in the name of God.
Sickened by grief's anniversary

and bloated with what I could not say,
I took off my Pirates hat and raised my head
as a plane sliced through the clear sky
above us, then I led them up the hill
where children were dancing.

HOLY WATER

The dirt road leading to our door
now a muddy stream, and rain still
falling. Baptism flatters us. Water
defines us. Trout idle against
the current in the wispy river's
clear high water.

My children must learn to swim.
Soccer? Optional. Baseball?
Optional. Holding hands? Preferred.
The moon's teary face reflected.
Drowning is the worst death,
I say with no authority.

How high will it rise? Can we
escape? What could we float
into a makeshift boat?
Wind throws rain under the door
onto the kitchen floor.

An altar boy, I gripped the aspergillum
like a microphone and whispered
obscene jokes in the sacristy.
We can't row a symbol or find Noah's ark.

My children have not been baptized.
They hate church, and I've only take them
twice. We're looking out our one big window
and holding each other tight. *Kick,
stroke.* We practice breathing.
Liquid time rises around us.

SOLSTICE WITH RASPBERRY

Remember the second s in solstice.
Remember the p in raspberry.
The first summer window opens
with all the nervous drama
of an obscene puppet show.

My daughter's drawing of the sun
alternating orange and yellow rays
anchors the solar system
across four sheets of paper
curling from the kitchen wall.

Last night I turned off the floodlight
and saw the first firefly ever
in my backyard at 3419 Parkview
in Pittsburgh. It flashed
in the city's half darkness.

One elusive light. Joy briefly
catchable. I said *hey* with all sincerity.
My daughter sings the opera
of her awakening. I envy
her sudden unspellable joy.

Yesterday she asked me,
What's the matter?
Worry's unpronounced letters
drift into dust motes. What do
young birds have to say
about the heart's perfect

misspellings, the lure of ripeness?
This morning she picks
the season's first red raspberry
and drops it on my cereal.
The solar system shudders.

THIMBLEBERRIES

Because the fruit is so soft, it does not pack or ship well, so thimbleberries are rarely cultivated commercially.

We spent that summer in Marquette in the UP
of MI with our two children, 4 and 5.

Fluky heat—our toes in Lake Superior
without freezing into pebbles. Offshore sat an island

I wanted to swim to, until told each year someone dies
doing just that. We had driven to one edge

of the country to mourn a sudden passing on the other,
to make a few bucks in the tourist trade

selling t-shirts that said "I Was Here."
We ate pasties, collected bright rocks and all things solid.

One day behind train tracks near our little stand,
we stumbled onto tart thimbleberries and found

the tender touch to pick them so they did not bleed.
The children did not need to bend or worry about thorns—

better than us, small hands quickly staining
my upturned hat forever. How many of us die

trying to swim to an island? We heard
you had to eat them right away, so we did.

STRING, JANUARY, SCHENLEY PARK, PITTSBURGH

Trudging beside me through snow,
my six-going-on-seven-year-old daughter says
she likes my sledding laugh and *why don't you
laugh more?* We've just descended on our rickety
sled, snow spraying up crystal joy.

Today I wrote the new year for the first time.
My son asked my age and measured my foot
with string. Two neighbors still Christmas-lit.
Our tree, planted in snow, waits for garbage day.

Tomorrow maybe I'll measure my life.
Cut the string and tape it to a piece of paper.
Or floss with it or use it as a bookmark.
Empty my penny jar into the bank's machine.
Count each of my wife's footsteps as a heartbeat.

This morning, I garbage-picked an old metal desk
for my children. Heavier than my entire family.
I wheeled it into the garage on our red wagon.
I can't lift it into the house. I'll wait for a friend
to visit. A big friend. Yesterday, a big old friend

I saw back in Detroit at Christmas wrote,
I wish we were still sitting around the table talking...
Sometimes I live on ellipses and the rotten music
of my youth. We'd debated the merits of Dylan's latest,
just like thirty years ago, as our kids disappeared

into the safe basement of their actual childhoods.
They put on a puppet show for us with paper bags.
We discussed the French and Indian War, internet stigmata,
and drugs we never had the nerve or chance to try.

My daughter likes my sledding laugh. It's all downhill,
so why pretend to steer? You can't just promise
to laugh more and have it happen. A string of lights.
The heart's ellipses connected with a piece of string.

MARTIN LUTHER KING, JR. DAY

My son boxes in our basement with Andre
in the enormous red gloves my father gave him
for Christmas. He is the Great White Hope

for soft blows and hard laughter beneath me.
A day off to dip strawberries in sugar,
then lick whatever sugar's left.

4° outside. Inside, no low blows, no clutching.
No rounds. No decision. A day to resist
easy messages as I sit in the kitchen listening,

making them a lunch that's too sweet,
but they're only nine—a little extra sugar now.

IN CASE OF EMERGENCY

My son said he felt sick
on Ryan Road in our dented blue Escort
on the way to visit my oldest friend.
Christmas, and we—*now*, he said.
I took off my hat. He leaned forward
from the back seat.

A year later, that car got totaled
in front of our house by a student
checking her phone, spring,
and in the yard I was turning over—
crash—I stumbled to the street:
blown airbags, burnt shock.

Tree branches sway tall in the wind.
My son, many states away now,
will not wear a hat. The next car,
a Villager, hit a deer one night, and—
looks like rain, what do you think?
Don't throw me a surprise party.

My oldest friend, a third-generation
upholsterer, just went bankrupt.
He works out of his garage
to try and keep his house.
Slow leaks, and then the flood.
My son on the phone wants to know,

did he do the right thing?
My wife pulls up the driveway
in our latest, an Escape.
She balled up the hat, threw it away,
and my ears were cold that Christmas
though my son felt better quickly.

Rain beats sudden against
the window. The next morning,
I found the deer, alive, lying
in the woods, eyes on mine.
I can't speak for anyone else
but I do. *Our hats*, I tell my son—

MIDDLE AGES

Last night I got out of bed
to find my son on the dark stairs
looking for me. He couldn't sleep,
hoped I'd still be awake.

Last week, I quizzed him
on the Middle Ages before his test.
We need more illuminated manuscripts,
I told him. And fewer lies.

Yesterday, the wall of wind
on the bridge over Panther Hollow
stung me into walking backward
with my eyes closed. It pressed me

against the railing and whispered
jump. December. A family of ducks
in the half-frozen pond below.
Golden panthers tarnished with chill
at both ends of the bridge.

How can we go nowhere
and everywhere at the same time?
That'll keep you up. Wind hissed
unhindered up the crease of the hollow.

Will the pond freeze over,
enough to skate on? Where will
the ducks go?

I have no magic dust, I told him,
my hand on his shoulder
as I led him back to bed.

Climbing up the dark stairs, I pressed
my feet hard to hear the creaking.
I felt my son's tender bones.

Someday he will never find me.

SAFETY LINES, SCHENLEY PARK

At the cancer festival, bald kids line up
for the hot-air balloon parked hillside
under a glorious untethered May sun.

Sunscreened, bouncy in new sneakers,
my son and daughter walk with me
in our T-shirts for a cure, *the* cure.

The route, a big loopy circle
like the handwriting of a novice
trying hard to impress.

On stage, shrill survivors give each other
prizes. The cancer kids in line, still,
waiting. They know the deal:

the balloon's thick ropes staked
to the ground. Wouldn't I be just
as shrill? Shriller?

URBAN EXPLORERS, SCHENLEY PARK

This morning in the concrete pond
we sailed toy boats where runoff
collects beneath Panther Hollow Bridge.
Three abandoned tires. One rat.

The Troubled Youth Brigade cleared trash
from the trail in their bright T-shirts,
a progressive dandelion chain gang
hip-hopping to imagined amplification.

The boats, mired in algae, listed in the heat
though we kept yanking their strings.
That boat needs a motor, one kid said.

My daughter collected muddy rocks
in her hat, insisting they'd be pretty
once she cleaned them up.

We squinted up under the bridge
at tangled strands of graffiti.
One kid claimed a tag we'd seen
around the city, impressing my son.

Wilted, we headed home.
One yellow shirt flashed us a gang sign.
Only the wildest flowers
survive this heat.

SLEEP/BALM

When my son was still a believer
in parental love and steady embrace,
I gave him sleep balm to rub
on his temples when he could not—
when he stirred with the lack of light
and dark space dizzied around him.

He believed in sleep balm
and thus drifted off to its menthol magic.
And when I entered later to listen
to him breathe—the rise and fall
of what sustains me too—
I thought I knew a few things.

*

He's outgrown the bedframe, flung
the mattress askew across the floor,
and what I smell and he does not
is the reek of pulling away. I hear him
storm the steps into early morning
on sleepless nights we share.
Rigid in my bed, afraid to find him
twinning my lack of dreams.

Sleep balm. Honey dreams.
A child's damp forehead.
A father, excommunicated,
remembers worship at the temples.

SMALL TALK

I screw the legs on the new kitchen chairs
backwards. My wife and I and our two teenagers

struggle to hold ourselves up during dinner's
weighted silence. No more sharing time,

silly silverware, or sippy cups.
We cannot force-feed them nostalgia's poison.

Under the table, our feet brace us against
this new burden pressing us down toward

each other. No one mentions the obvious.
We're on four failing rockets, nothing

to do but mumble last words to outer space.
They know everything, yet are descending

with us. I realize my mistake, but keep it
to myself. I grip the sides of my chair.

Well, I say. *What did you kids do today?*

ON OUR ANSWERING MACHINE BOB PLAYS THE HARMONICA

He took one class, enough to learn
"Happy Birthday." If you get on his list,
he'll call to serenade you. My daughter
turned fourteen yesterday, on the list
from year one. Today I play her the message,

Bob's plaintive wail. He retired last year.
Sold his tiny house, moved into a tinier,
more decrepit one after a neighbor
kidnapped his dog. A long, sad story,
now part of the tune. My daughter

eats a snack, trailing crumbs, ignoring
the sentiment. It's not like he's the latest
teen sensation. She knows it's the old guy
with the dog, garden, small house—not
the smaller. She'll never visit the new one.

She leaves the room before the notes melt away.
Alone, Bob throws his own birthday parties.
Curiosity may have killed one cat,
but it also made friends with some other cats,
and that one dead cat, it was an accident,

I'd tell my daughter, if she were still in the room.
Bob's one of those off-the-leash types,
and his neighbor—I said I wouldn't get into it.
"Happy Birthday," then a soft click. I'll tell him
she loved it. That she's always loved it,

will love it forever. What I remember
about fourteen could fill a thin book called *Me*—
everyone else, just footnotes crabbed
across the bottom of the page. One day,
further down the future's long trail

of missed phone calls and grim messages,
runaway dogs and sad parties,
will she remember Bob playing for her?
Alone in the sudden silence
of the kitchen, I press *Repeat Message*.

MAN WITH CHILD, MAY

Under deep gray thunderless skies
a man cradles an infant to his bare chest
on the long swoop of spotty grass
in the tiny park across the street.

Pre-dawn—the child silent, the father
silent, bare feet bending
tender grass, the world's mouth
gently enclosing them.

I can't say what the three deer
on the edge of the clearing think, alert
at the wet rustle of dew. Nor the man,
idling down the block, plopping

a paper onto every porch.
I'm going to say the father
has taken the child outside
to let the mother sleep.

I have stood where the man
has stood. Today at the window,
I watch the green unfolding dawn,
waiting for my own man-child
who did not come home last night.

Sleepless swatch of sweat-thick hair,
bristle beard, pale, tattooed bicep,
beltless jeans-sag. The child?
Blue blanket and a light tuft of hair.

Its warm breath
against the man's shoulder
thaws the goddamned world.

LAST NIGHT I DROVE MY SON HOME

from his friend's house, where they were filming
a movie starring my son in a love triangle—
fifteen, he's never been in a love right angle,
or even a love straight line, as far as I know.
He stopped talking two years ago—to me, I mean.
I got this secondhand from a street informant
I'll refer to by her code name, Little Sister.

Warm night, windows rolled down—
my cheap car requires physical cranking.
(Not even a CD player!) Purchased back when
he was ten and still kissed me goodnight
and may even have held my hand
as we watched old movies. (No cable TV!)
Yesterday he made me kill a giant bug,
and I briefly saw that ten-year-old again.

Full moon—I saw him look up at it, following
it as I turned and we lost it to the trees.
September, but moist like August. In that silence
I ached for a few soft words between us.

On a sidewalk near the park a young man sat,
face in hands. A friend stood helpless above him.
I slowed down. *What's that guy doing?* I said aloud.
Is he OK?
      I see him too, my son said.
As the friend helped the man to his feet, I sped on.

My son hummed an old song about the moon
I didn't know he knew. My son, the star
of a movie I'll never see. I just get
these vague coming attractions.
I caught him in a lie or two last week.
Every exchange a house of cards—all it takes
is a deep sigh, and they tumble down.

I'd have hummed along with him,
but I didn't want him to stop.

GOOD TEETH, SPRING BREAK

Last week I took my kids to the dentist.
Want to hear about it? Or has your watch
already stopped?

If you want to hear about bad sex,
see page 32. A loss of limb?
Pages 44 to 46.

The three of us get in the car
with shiny rinse-and-spit teeth.
The sun's doing that coy little thing

where it says, you didn't think
I was coming back, did ya?
Like it doesn't know

we've been dying down here.
Welcome back, dude, we're saying,
licking our clean teeth.

My daughter says,
going to the dentist's not so bad
and my son says, yeah, that lady

who cleans your teeth is nice,
and my daughter says, yeah,
she said my teeth are so perfect

she'd like to take pictures to show
all her patients. The kids, 14 and 15,
so it's not some cute little awwwww

story where they get a balloon
or a smiley-face sticker, though we do
get floss and a toothbrush

from the peppy hygienist
who must've been a cheerleader
or an exclamation point in another life—

she made even me smile, dancing
around the chair to the greatest hits
of the 70s, 80s, and 90s. Though I don't like

those hits, I could hold my mouth open
forever for a woman like that.
I hope that's not a yawn I see out there,

but if so, the torrid affair's on page 62.
Here, we're in the middle of a minor
miracle, my children talking happily

in the presence of he-who-must-not-be-
named unless something is explicitly
desired by those who cannot drive

yet. I'm so (secretly) thrilled by this
that I take them to Subway (yes,
they asked) for lunch. This odd

emergence of parens so late
can only be explained by the fact
that I may have lost everybody else

by now, so I feel like I'm talking to myself.
If you're still with me, wave your hand,
cough, or (what the hell) shake

a tail feather. We drove home
with the windows down.

PHOTO OPS: WHERE EMPATHY BEGINS

My daughter rode the camel but refused to ride
the elephant. In Qatar at fifteen, she lobbied hard
for the camel till I drove miles into the desert

to find one. A man under an umbrella took my riyals
and joined us in the hot sand to slowly lead her up
and back the short track other tourists

had stomped flat. She posed, I clicked, and all
was well, the rutted world smoothed and shrunken
into cliché. We hurried back to the Land Rover's AC.

Three years later, on a government trip to Sri Lanka,
she was taken by her leader to a slop pit where a man
took their rupees, then beat the elephant till it rose,

then beat it again while the group took turns, one
by one, on top of the thin, sickly creature. Her leader
cursed my daughter when she refused to climb.

She had seen into the dark moons of the elephant's eyes
and felt its enormous shame. Her leader argued
that she had paid in advance for all of them. Empathy

does not lend itself to photos. I just have the currency
of her words. *It cost so much*, her leader yelled,
you're ruining it for everyone, but she could not beat

my daughter into rising.

GROWTH CHART

I want to measure my children by hands
      like they did in the old days—

in that inexact human way,
      measure them against what I imagined

when I could hold them both in my arms.
      But they are too big

for their father's weepy calculations,
      his clumsy dance of letting go.

The man who sold us this house
      left us two yardsticks in the closet

and countless tulips in the garden.
      When he died, I missed his obit,

busy, I suppose, waving a flag in the wind
      for my children, signaling the heavens

like they did in the old days.

I don't want to talk shop
or I'll end up with the hollowed-out,
lead-filled billy clubs I made in Shop class.

> I briefly had a small business.
> The hoods called it "The Jimbo"
> and paid me good cash moolah
> right there in Shop while Mr. Stooch
> sat stupored in his office swigging
> from his magic bottomless cup
> of the unspoken, preparing
> a hand basket for his trip to hell—
> his own private woodworking project.

But three times I have been asked
to nominate or endorse people
for genius awards. First thing
I thought of was "The Jimbo."

No, first thing was "What about me?"
But I duly nominated and recommended
like any dutiful middle-aged mid-list *shlup*.
If I was a genius, I would know how to spell that,
or at least look it up to find out if it is indeed
a word. Or, just by using it, I'd find my usage
cited in the latest genius dictionaries.

I never tasted sour grapes, but I tasted
sour wine and drank it, drank everything,
until I quit drinking entirely. It didn't take
a genius to know I should've quit years
earlier. Sometimes sobriety itself
is a form of genius. Right, genius?

I nominated this young hotshot
whose debut prose rose off the page
as if carved by one of those fancy saws
we had to get special permission to use.

> I liked Shop—stepping outside
> for a smoke with the hoods
> who occasionally and affectionately

punched me in the shoulder
while I affectionately tried not to wince.

Mr. Stooch was not his real name.
If he emerged from his windowed office
more often, I might've remembered it.
We affectionately called him "OD"
for "Old Drunk." Oh, we were full
of affection on that sawdust
and metal shaving littered floor.

I swore that, despite his early success,
it would absolutely not go to his head—
his neck was so thick, how could it get
through there?
        If you get early success like that
you might need a "The Jimbo" to gently
conk yourself in the head once in a while
to stunt its *inflatability*—can you believe that's
not a word? It wants me to change it to *infallibility*,
and maybe that's correct. I should have had
my mother-in-law bake him one of her famous
Humble Pies.
        He starts carving his own name
instead of more genius-type words—he makes
one Capital I after another—it's all
he can make anymore,
        and Mr. Smooch(?)
might've been the only one left who could still
stand him because he'd be filling Mr. Scooch(?)'s
cup with the strong stuff of his own ego,
allowing him to pretend to listen
while getting completely hammered.

I found myself rooting for him *not* to be
a Genius. Though the Genius Foundation
complimented me on the subtle middle-
brow-ness of my nomination, Wiser Heads
prevailed, as they sometimes do, but not often
enough, and he didn't get one.
        Yet Wiser Heads
let Mr. Spooch continue on till retirement
because he was *so close*—
        and as I approach

Retirement and introduce myself, hollering
out across the distance, Hey Mr. R, I'm a comin'
yer way! Wait for me! (Don't kill me off
when I can nearly taste your sweet languor,
or at least get a whiff of it—fresh sawdust
to enhance my soft-shoe toward death.)

        Mr. Mooch was examined by the Prevailing
        Wiser Heads for allowing the proliferation
        of "The Jimbo" under his unwatchful eye
        because Parker, famous enough to go
        by one name, like all the Big Stars,
        was found in possession of a "The Jimbo"
        by the Local Authorities (who to be honest
        had very few Wiser Heads and nary a Genius)
        when they stopped him for crashing
        his Transportation Special through the Rec Center's
        locked gates because damn it, he needed
        a place to Park.
                Parker survived two years
        in the Navy only to come back and finish school
        because his mother was a mean sombitch
        who demanded it.
                Parker, good-natured about it,
        and not without affection, and blind drunk to boot,
        explained enthusiastically to the Officers
        where he got "The Jimbo"
        and *that kid's a damn genius.*

        I was temporarily decommissioned
        by the Wiser Heads, though they did not
        make me join the Navy, where I'd have
        sunk like a lead-filled billy club,
        so for that I am eternally and affectionately
        grateful. We had odd ways of showing
        our affection. I hope no "Jimbos"
        were used in a display of one of those ways,
        but to be honest, I know otherwise.

The hot air balloon of affection. It's all science.
How could I have thought he'd be immune?
When you're a celebrity in the parade, you should
at least toss your own candy to the crowd, right?
Not hire some *schloop* to do it for you?

None of us come out looking good, I know,
        but I can't decide the greater shame
in all this—it's a story problem, the kind I always
        got wrong and thus got relegated to Shop 1
and Shop 2, where my true genius was revealed.
        Just ask any of the smiling smokers
leaning against the school wall, squinting into spring sun,
        the whole notion of a "The Jimbo," just a pleasantry
to be exchanged against those warm, humble bricks
        where some of us may have sprayed
our secret names, for who among us could kick anybody's
        ass in that Land of Pleasantry, stolen moments,
without consequence,
        all of us geniuses
                when it came to that?

HEAT OF DEPARTURE

Ninety degrees of thick, rude heat—a summer guest
we can't get rid of—hovering over our city,

our brick house. Yet our son who's leaving home
tomorrow, we wish would stay. No AC in his room,

but a window unit in ours for wicked waves like this.
He's almost 18. *Can't sleep*, he says, and, though

we've offered before, now he quickly slips
his mattress on the floor in our room and plops

down. 6'5". His own room wrecked with packing.
His last three nights, a man sprawled back

into a boy before us. *The heat*, we all keep
saying, *it's awful*. In the morning I rise early

and turn off the AC
just to hear him breathing.

UPDATE ON/ELEGY FOR THE HERE AND NOW

For those of you keeping score at home,
that's four marriages of twenty-plus years
ground up, compacted, composted,
abandoned in the last three months of school.
Yet, ninth grade exams go on.

The auditorium shrinks into a swollen mob
for Honors Day. Our daughter in it some-
where, checking her best friend's parents
off the list as they sit on separate sides of discretion.

The referees toss their weepy tear-soaked flags,
late and inconsequential, then pick them up
off the empty field, slinking to the special room
under the stands where you don't have to take
sides. But that door's always locked.

They remain prisoners, exposed.
Does that merit a red card? Can I now
quit the game? Whatever you call it,
it's blood sport. The ninth graders are layering
on mascara, disappearing in the park,
stealing what they can while losing everything

in the gap between the new locations
where it's never a home game. Don't you love
the inadequacy of sports metaphors?
We lock our doors, program in new numbers
to track our own kids down. The vaccine is scarce,
out of stock, invisible, with side effects,

but we're taking multiple doses in lieu
of renewing our vows—which is like—I'm sorry
for going there again—the vote of confidence
from the owner just before the coach gets fired.
How about a tune-up, new spark plugs, how about
if we kick each other's tires for luck? But tonight,

what do we do with this girl weeping on our steps,
stoned out of her young mind, wanting, just
wanting a ride back to her impossible home?

THE ALONE-DOORS

Don't try this at home.
Try this on a wet dark road
with an unpromising destination—
hospital / funeral / prison—
or on just another useless errand
created by badly transcribed directions
for the good life
when all your calculations wash away
in the smear of steady rain
softly eroding the names of those you once
called *best friend* with all the sincerity
of a big-haired rock star on his first arena tour.

List the memories no one can confirm,
the alone-doors with the one key
spiked in your palm, burning off the acid
of nostalgia, tattooing the soft skin with loss
when all you want is to get it in the door
and turn and enter and witness again:

weeds behind the garage swaying tall
against the mesh fence like the long hair
of a girl you think you love
who will die with her braces on.
The neighbor's dog, belly swollen
with anonymous puppies, eyes softening
as you pet her pressed up against the fence.

The puppies disappear. The dog
disappears. You burn trash in a rusty barrel
and ash rises in the gray Detroit spring,
the last patch of snow in the angle of shade,
and the sundial of your young life
turns out to be a chalk drawing
by the deaf-mute down the block
who kicked your ass once—why? Why?
Memories recede like the line of snow.

A rubber ball bounces against a wall
and returns, bounces, returns. A wounded
sparrow hops crooked near the curb,
and you should find a way to put it out

of its misery but/but/but—the ball bounces,
returns, the comfort of the wall
and its resistance, sky spiraling
into dusk, then night, and you're aiming
for the one brick, the perfect strike,
cheating for yourself, you alone
against brick, time, and a dying sparrow
waiting for a cat, watching you with a hard eye,
its silent intrusion into the rest of your life.

Punished, you bent over the furnace vent
in the floating dust of the silent house.
The others all at the fall festival
and its traveling carnival of greasy rides
and sincere flirting. You, caught in a lie,
a twisted net of deceit your clumsy fingers
could not unravel, and all you have
is the furnace clicking on, and, hunched over,
you hog the heat, dismissing all other forms

of prayer. What did you lie about? Why did he
hit you? Who rode the Tilt-A-Whirl with that girl?
Hot breath whispered against your face,
into your hollow chest, your eyes closed,
listening. Are you still with me,
or are you nudging whoever's next to you,
tilting your head toward the exit?

The authority of the speaker has left
the building. I admit the deceit
of instructions leading nowhere
but to my alone-door where I will greet you
like the invisible friend you imagined
for two weeks during a bad stretch.

I have been practicing my coffee-stained
smile and my knee-worn patience
in front of the vacated jury of my peers
just for you. I have dreamt the world's
most comfortable chairs for us to sit in.
Listen, you will say. *Remember?* I'll say.

LIGHTEN UP, BUT WATCH YOUR HEAD

Today I feel as vulnerable as a peanut butter
and jelly sandwich in a fold-over—not Ziploc—
bag inside a paper bag scrawled with my initials
smeared across Eight Mile Road, dropped by
a bedraggled boy, stoned for high school—
the better to sleep through, my dear—

and he's laughing at that so hard his eyes
are tearing—he's already late, but that's okay—
and the sandwich? That's okay too. No books?
A joke of epic proportions. So, why's he even
going? You should have asked him before
he got stoned. *Walk/Don't Walk.* Hilarious.

Today, pushing sixty, in for all the tests,
having fasted since midnight as instructed,
I check all the boxes. They can see a lot
of things these days they couldn't see
back then. But they can't see that boy.

and wear a baseball hat with a patch
of that animal sewn onto it. I will touch
the animal every so often to make sure
I've still got my hat on.

I want to be in a club named for an animal
that meets in a cinder block clubhouse
that smells like that animal. I will memorize
all of the rules and learn how to make

that animal sound. I want to be in a club
named for an animal and march in parades
dressed as that animal and throw Tootsie
Rolls at bratty kids who shout

you don't look like a real animal!
So, will you be my animal?

HEARING LOSS IN LATE MIDDLE AGE

Every sentence that begins
    is unfinished.

By the time we start listening
    to our bodies

we're half-deaf. *Speak up!*
    we tell the body,

the body hoarse
    with the torn metal

of grief, the thick mucus
    of all we've choked

back. The sentence of our life
    will finish itself.

If God isn't our witness,
    who is? The body?

What? What? How many times
    can you ask without

paralysis? Height and weight.
    Why don't they rhyme?

We begin and end with statistics
    and in between is all—

is all, what? Not poetry.
    The improvised dancing

to the heart's jazz—
    you're faking it,

dancing to nothing.

THE MIDDLE AGES

We're tipping over like hollow trees, our roots rising, shaggy with dirt. Have we missed the storm that did the damage? What's lifted us into brittle clock hands, whittled us into slivers, rocked our boats into murky numbness? Are we not soldiers in the active army, are we not fluent in the language of moist passage? The questions twist us into unpleasant doubts, the humpbacked crones of simple children's stories. If we are both passengers, then who is steering, who has worn the brakes down to metal on metal? Our horns, weak, mournful. We scratch our bark against each other and our teeth fall out, and it's worse than our bite because suddenly all our bills are dutifully paid. Nothing left to forgive or save for, our traveler's license expired. Our frayed strings no longer bind us to shore, but the wind has died and the current swirls in on itself. We are all vehicle and no tenor. Timber! Fore! The house of cards, the improvisational landscapes of unmapped dreams, solidified into fortresses and long, straight roads. Our combinations are memorized. We fill out forms with dulled pencils and sharp erasers. I had an accident today! Did you hear the weather! If we're trees, why do both spring and autumn ignore us? We're on a rocket ship in a movie from the fifties. How will we ever get back to earth? How will we even get off the ground? Someone's taking a chainsaw to our framed photographs on the mantel. Just sweep up when you're done, you say, or I say, or we both say, our voices drowning in mad, polite fury.

SLICING CELERY

I'd rather go blind than to see you walk away
—Etta James

I enter the house to find my blind mother
sitting at the kitchen table next to her walker
slicing celery by feel, pulling a knife length-
wise through stalks, straight toward her thumb.

Butchered celery scattered on the counter,
sites of previous engagements with the enemy.
She's making chicken salad with a rotisserie
bird from the supermarket, its stripped

and battered carcass strewn across another
battlefield. For me, though I told her I'd bring
dinner. As wobbly as a rubbery stalk forgotten
in the crisper drawer, she pushes up to greet me.

I'd rather not go blind. I take away the knife
and grasp her hands. She's rambling about having
something to offer. I've brought Chinese takeout
and the sweet iced tea she likes. She reaches up

to touch my face. I smell fresh green stalks.
We pull the knife toward us.

YELLING FIRE

My mother's metal walker drifted
       into the fire station driveway
overshooting the entrance
       to her condo complex.

Blind, she wheeled from grass edge
       to grass edge across the wide cement arc
like a remote control car,
       like a dog trapped by its invisible fence,

like a blind woman panicked
that any moment a fire truck might erupt
out the station's garage doors
and mow her down.

Fifty yards away, salvation—the irony
       of an old melodrama.
Where is the hero who will wheel
       her horse to safety?

I keep trying to find escape—
       for her, this. What's
a blind woman doing out alone
       in August wilt?

She tells me the story
on the phone that night.
       My father shouts in the back-
       ground, *Tell him who saved you!*

       Someone leading her out
of the cement plot and back to the condo,
       someone with an unseen accusing stare
as he ushers her in, like she's a teenager

who stayed out all night or a runaway dog.
Like his wife of sixty years
who will never leave him.
       Yet she tries. A short walk alone,

and she's failed that. Exhausted,
she falls into memories of my childhood.

My father, embarrassed and deaf,
raises the volume on the remote.

It's too late for Braille
        or a GPS heart. She accidentally
hangs up, and I wait for her to call back.
                I am still waiting.

And if you're feeling sorry for her about now,
        my father'd like a few words with you.
He still has faith in breadcrumbs the birds ate
        erasing the path they'd mapped out long ago

leaving only shame enough for everyone.
        Burnt toast—black crumbs rim her mouth.
        Soon he'll never find her. And me,
why didn't I call her back?

I shout *fire, fire,* in the crowded theater
        but no one panics except me,
the only one who sees the nearest lighted exit
        going up in flames.

THE PREDICTABLE NATURE OF TRAGEDY

Nine children, and they all smoked.
One dog, and it bit.

A house of reliable clouds and volatile mirages.
One father, and he reigned. He rained

down blows. He snatched their cigarettes.
One mother, and she abandoned the church,

set up shop at a local bar owned by—
it gets messy here—everybody related

by betrayal—and the kids—which one
set the fire? Five dead, wife too.

Her alibi did her in. Four children
remain, and they all failed math.

The father—perhaps he shouldn't be drunk too—
passed out in his car outside the plant

while the walls of his house collapsed
in a cataclysmic crash amidst the flashing lights

of God's—no, leave God out of it.
We stood in the street in pajamas and jackets

barely and forever hearing her scream
in that anarchic orchestra of flames.

You can fill in the blanks so easily it'll tear
you apart. Stop, rewind, cycle backwards

down the ho-hum street past the house
with the nine kids—and ain't they cute,

every damned one of them?

A mob of drunk college kids stole
my Support Our Troops/Stop the War
sign Friday night and marched down
the street chanting some slur I could not
decipher, curled at the cold window,
smoking the glass.

A young, coatless girl, long blond hair
streaming, stumbled past in tight jeans.
In school, I never thought about Vietnam
but would've done anything to get inside
those jeans—yank up a sign, cuss out
some old fart, take a side she took.

Early November, and still, one brilliant tree
flames in the park. Friday night, she was
that tree. Saturday morning, I find my sign
torn among red beer cups and random trash
on the steps of the party house.

I ring the bell, pound the door, hoping that,
hungover, they won't kick my ass.
It's *Mister* Old Fogey to you, buster.
No one answers. Young people *for* war?

I tape my sign together, stick it back
in the ground. Democracy sometimes means
as much as the word *interesting*. I haven't
been stoned in a dozen years, but I want
to get stoned. To be a flaming tree.

Who messed with the on-off switch,
the horizontal hold? Those kids too young
to know that knob, yet old enough
to be *Over There* right now. Bring *those* kids
home so they can get drunk and commit
small random acts of destruction.

I'd take that, I decide, walking away
from debris, heading to the park
to look at that tree one more time
before the leaves fall.

I LOVE DIRTY PUSSY *GRAFFITIED*

on the Jersey barrier
where the bike trail veers
sharp from Greenfield
to 2nd Avenue, forcing you to
slow down, take a long look.

Each time I make the turn,
the words assault me.
What's graffiti's payoff
for the crass or inscrutable?

I approach that blind curve,
ring my bell to alert anyone
headed my way. The sleek kits
of faux racers mock my bell
with stealth-passing, no word
or warning.

I'm only out to get my grizzled
exercise. I'd sell you ice cream
and innocence if I could stabilize
the weight, though back in the age
of acne, I myself was flying
over handlebars, crass, inscrutable.

Today, cloudy Sunday threat
hovering. I make the turn, and:
I Love PUrty PussyCATS.
It doesn't take much to twist
the world into something half-
sweet. It rains, it pours,

this old man doesn't snore,
doesn't play knick-knack
on your door. This old man
makes the turn. Rings his bell.

are swept away with the clink-
and-blink tune of the happy drunk,
plates piled and carried inside
to harden into morning reckoning,
we form a ragged ring around a fire
in an inverted manhole, its thick circle
perfect for our purpose, and for all
who believe in the limitations
of ritual and a healthy layer of rust.

Three couples who've raised our kids
and seen them flee as if we ourselves
were flames. Six of us swaying
in the in-between we don't talk about,
tilting toward ash ourselves.

We don't roast anything or sing off-key
dirges of nostalgia—is the fallen sky
glowing or glaring? A friend's chair breaks,
and he sets it in flames without comment.
He remains standing. *Please remain standing.*
Please be seated. Please genuflect before
your own burning coffin. Please do not listen
to italicized voices ever again.

The mood among us—the moon among us—
oh, we almost love each other.
We will be polite about dying: *You first.*
After you. Please. We will make gracious
gestures, miming the executioner's prayer.

The chair remains upright, flames curling
around its rungs like something Biblical,
or maybe just the end of a long life—
I mean, night. Long night. *Isn't he*
dead yet? somebody says. I think it's me.
And someone falls back, laughing
and crying. It might be my wife.
The bench I sit on is not broken,
but I rise to toss it on the flames.

BRUSHING TEETH WITH MY SISTER AFTER THE WAKE

at my kitchen sink, the bathroom upstairs
clogged with family from out of town

spending the night after the wake
and the after-wake—cold beverages

have been consumed and comfort food,
leftovers bulging both the fridge

and the minifridge. In our fifties, both
half-asleep half-awake, we face each

other. My sister's smile foams white
down her chin at the end of a day

on which no one has smiled. We laugh.
We may never brush our teeth together again.

No mirror down here to see our haggard faces.
We rinse, we spit. As we were taught.

TAKING PAINKILLERS AFTER SURGERY

The lion and lamb cancel each other out
in the land of painkillers. Something sticky
in the brain canals, and the cleaning boats
with their electric snakes are on strike.

My battered knees sing the blues,
kicked out of church for smart-alecky
prayers, last-minute conversions
and perversions and alternate versions

of an earlier life. They changed the test
right when I thought I'd finally figured
it out. You wouldn't shoot a three-legged
dog, would you, Jesus?

I took too many time-killers, fiddling
with radio stations while love burned.
If the fog lifts, give me my eyeballs back.
If the fog lifts, whisper sweet static in my ear.

Tell me a bedtime story about crutches
and the witch who rides them.
The lion and the lamb share a private joke.
Tell me that joke.

ON SEEING AN AERIAL VIEW OF THE PEACE MARCH

January 26, 2003
Five thousand people marched slushy streets under a steady snowfall
yesterday in the culmination of a weekend of anti-war events in
Pittsburgh.

Afterward, streets choke again
with cars and cabs and delivery trucks
as if we had never marched
over those white and yellow lines.

*

Fred and I sit in a diner drinking coffee
that scalds the roof off our mouths.
Snow melts quiet blotches into our jackets,
then the blotches evaporate.

*

The anarchists still wander, anxious
to be noticed, to punctuate the rage
that roils inside us—or maybe
they're just young and clueless.

*

How did *Peace March* get yanked
into Dismissive Sneer? We swill
our heat in silence, politely grizzled,
edges rounded into the proximity
of harmlessness. Yet we too linger.

*

Traffic, bulky, rude, and unyielding,
recaptures control, filling lanes
with metal menace—the idle of power.

Gas, brake, gas, brake, behind the police
reopening or reclosing, depending
on your pedestrian nature. A pregnant
woman wades past—gentle clouds
of her erupting smile.

*

You might call that manipulative,
but there she is, pausing at a red light.
Little harmonica notes surround her
like summer's gentle bees. She's smiling
at no one and everyone. The light changes
according to a system of timing and order.

*

Thousands of us—who counted?— marched
down 5th Avenue. I never chant. Fred does.
I like the simple shuffle and scrape of feet.
Snow drifted thick in slow fat flakes.
If I told you we looked beautiful
in that cool confetti honoring only
our presence, would you say I skewed
the figures? Oh, the heart's muted math.
Coffee's cold, and we have not said
a word, old friend.

*

My own daily cruelties and penances
and petty lies, temporarily at bay, stuffed
into salt-stained gloves and under the knit hat
colored with the flag of somebody's country.

The pregnant woman pulls herself up onto a bus.
Soon, she'll be blessing someone with a name.
Wet footprints under our table. Gas, brake,
gas, brake. Lights turn without us.

*

March 20, 2003. To freshen the shame
of reference. To turn on the TVs of memory
and despair, to walk away again
from the rigged game, pockets empty
with spite.

*

At the end, young protesters held a die-in
on cold wet concrete in the middle of 5th.
Fred and I have no interest in even
pretending to die. They looked real,
sprawled into elegant shapes as snow
kaleidoscoped down on them.

*

And if I say those flakes were the largest, softest
flakes ever, you might say I'm exaggerating.
And if I say you had to have been there,
you might say I'm copping out. I've given up
worrying what you think, truth set aflame,
stomped on like a cruel trick.

*

Two months later, the callous crew announced
Shock and Awe, and I clicked off my radio,
hung my head, pushed in a cracked cassette
of two old men joyfully acoustic with blues
to keep me on the road. In the dusty light
of calm dark, I imagined our voices carving
a wistful song about peace.

*

We drifted like snow on the closed-off street,
marching in ragged non-formations
while some took pictures and some took notes,
but most of us just made footprints
for disappearance. Snow melted against
our faces like tears, but we did not cry.

*

Not yet, crying. Not yet, dying.
We absorbed the blessing of snow
as we marched, our breath blending
with the breath of thousands
against what we knew was coming.
Then, the streets of war opened again.

A BRIEF HISTORY OF EVOLUTION

God carved his name in cement.
Then somebody took the carving stick

and stuck it through the heart of somebody
who disagreed. Then somebody else

took the stick and created the first museum
and charged admission to see the stick.

Then they started in on the cement.
Who owned it? One court ruled

it was vandalism. Then a dog pissed
on the judge's leg. But I get ahead of myself.

Those who made the cement demanded
crucifixion in lieu of community service.

It's the government's cement, the upper court
ruled. Then jackhammered it to smithereens.

Then The Smithereens formed a rock band.
Then God yanked off his fake beard

and danced on the head of a pin
while angels hissed and booed.

Perhaps I have this wrong. Hell broke loose
but they had a roundup. They sent out

a posse for God. Then God turned into a fish,
like they always said he would.

Swam away. And like that.

THE SYMMETRY OF DEPRESSION

I took a course in Sadness and got
an Incomplete. So did everyone else,
despite the grading curve arcing
into a rainbow on the blackboard—
or whiteboard, I can't recall.

I took a cure for Sadness. Canoe-shaped
Happy Pills to steer around swirling sink-
holes with names like Pure Screaming Hell
and Endless Pit of Despair. The guide,
a white-trash shape-shifter, fluent
in Rottweiler and Pit Bull.

I took a curve in Sadness
when I should have swung
for the fences. I joined a support group
for Contact Hitters, but they ejected me
for bringing in a loaded bat.

I downshifted to Okay Pills
and started throwing knucklers
and relying on the unreliability of wind.
The syllabus was blank and blue.
The take-home final continues to this day.

This day my bare March tree is angry
enough to 3D through my window.
I am erasing a treatise on spring.
Sweating out the vacuum-sucked color
of sky with the heat of friction.
I hear God loading his gun.

Didn't the radio just play that song?
The hits keep coming in increased doses.
Want to be in my study group?
I'll be our scribe. First, let me blow
away the pink eraser shreds
and make a wish.

SLIGHT

Yesterday a mourning dove
in the middle of Panther Hollow Road
did not rise as expected.

I twisted in my seat to see
a flurry of feathers settling,
and jolted into a pothole

dug by winter salt dripping
from the Forbes overpass.

Today I scrutinize the front grille
on my Focus: nothing.
If sacraments could be that fast,

perhaps we could all be forgiven
daily. I didn't swerve.

No great message here.
I just wanted to tell you about
those feathers falling behind me,

another small shrug.
Nobody turned to salt,
nobody saved.

TEACHING THE SPIDER TO FLY

I sat at the long table for our panel presentation.
Bottles of water placed in front of each chair
like toy guns. Words heavy in late afternoon
sunk, hovering over the floor like low fog
before rain. Bodies around me twisted into
bad posture, then settled. The moderator caught
my eye and pointed to a large spider on our table.

We were supposed to talk about our plans
for the future. The audience was supposed to be
interested. Los Angeles, where they might not get
much fog. Much rain. I don't know what
most people do with spiders, but I flicked it
onto the floor in the middle of the square
of conference tables. The moderator frowned
to indicate that in the future I should gently lower
spiders to the floor. My future was at stake.

At home in Pittsburgh, one of the few roles
granted to me by my teenage children
is to kill bugs. One tissue, one *squish*.
I thought it was okay to send that spider
to a soft carpet landing. To those who are now
frowning, I'd prefer that to a tissue,
and to the condescending paper-to-carpet release.
Just imagine somebody flicking you off
the table, sending you flying.

Couldn't that be wonderful? I wanted to ask,
but my time had already expired on the panel
on the futuring of future meetings to further
feature the future in which much is uncertain
in the drone of late afternoon. The fog was rising
above our heads, so some began to stand.
I remained seated, taking notes
in my spidery scrawl.

JIM DANIELS MISSES HIS TEN-CENT TIP AS HE PREPARES FOR AN UNPLEASANT MEETING

I began the day attempting to balance my checkbook
and looking on-line at *Property Matches for Jim Daniels*.
I wish I could light those matches over a bowl
of hash. I smell the sweet burn even now.

I began the day with nostalgia for being stoned
while reading email messages from the Gospel Choir
of Whiners. The matches don't match my checkbook.
I wish I could light those checks like a—

no, I've got no nostalgia for crack, the soul's
chemical burn. I'm off by 90 cents,
the amount I collected from customers
each week on my paper route.

Some let me keep the dime, some didn't.
No apparent rhyme or treason to it.
I thought all poetry rhymed back then
and only sissies and brainiacs understood

or cared about it. I wish I could endorse
my checks with poems instead of *Jim Daniels*.
I wish for more checks that need endorsing.
Today, I'm not drinking coffee fast enough

to keep it hot. Zapping it in the microwave,
I burn it bitter in the magic machine.
I loved that simple job: pickup and delivery,
the controlled wild fling of paper

onto porch. It's time to head in to the office
for another concert by the Whiners. I still love
The Clash. They pulled my hair out by the roots
without apology. They didn't mope, nope.

And you could dance to their controlled wild
flings, and the next morning wake to the buzz
of loss in your ears, glorious human loss.
You hear me, Jim Daniels?

I was at the president's house for a thank-you reception. I was being thanked. We were all being thanked. Nervous about being thanked. How dressed up should we get to be thanked? I wore my blue blazer, a hand-me-down from my son who outgrew it and me both. I kept the blazer on over my wrinkled shirt. Sweat dribbled over my ribs. While the president made remarks, I was first in line at the faux pas buffet. Loading up, oblivious. I could be blackballed for my hunger now. I don't drink anymore—I used to be first in the bar line. I was amusing until I wasn't. Now, I just belch. I tried to slip out, my cheeks stuffed with multiple desserts, but I ran into dual harrumphers who seemed dismayed at my rapid exit. But I'm leaking, I wanted to say. I muffled something about the lovely weather and *how 'bout those Steelers* and strode, yes, strode, down the long circular drive and onto the click-clockety sidewalk in my magic shoes of discomfort worn special for the occasion so I could look down and admire them instead of making small talk with other honored thankees. I was off, down the now-dark street of houses few and far between with mulched money spread over the lawns. Or so it appeared in lieu of moonlight. I decided on a shortcut through the park—though I knew only the abstract notion of as-the-crow-flies shortcut— crashed into the woods thinking I should have brought my emergency crank flashlight the blind association gave me for my donation to my mother's blindness. Why had no one made a path for such an obvious shortcut for lost golf ballers and furtive lovers from the nearby college of which my president was president, and what had I done to deserve his thanks? I'd danced a soft-shoe in my hard shoes, I'd spoken *testing testing* into the holy microphone. I did bird calls and corny jokes. I took my seat and counted the bodies. It was an honor to be a thankee. A select group from the big group who deserved the buffet line. Where do you put your drink while you're standing and trying to eat off your tiny plate? I slopped salsa on the floor and casually rubbed it into the dark carpet. Why did I begin sprinting through the woods? The leaves had lost their trees and slickened beneath my feet. I ran into a bare black branch and split my lip. I thrashed and stumbled through the under- and over- brush. I sucked the blood so I would not bleed onto my fat tie or my wrinkled shirt or my blue blazer. Would I ever be invited to the President's Residence again? I was thinking that'd be a good song title for my next album when I suddenly emerged from the woods into a clearing of wet grass where I lay down and felt my heart beat as the cold soaked through my flexible slacks, my practical khakis. I heard a rustling through the trees. I closed my eyes and began my song.

MUSEUM OF BETRAYAL

The exhibits are covered with black cloth
      and aluminum foil
and must be viewed with pornographic glasses
      available in the gag gift shop.
The guide locked in the bathroom tunnels out
      to tell you the museum is closed
for renovation. He sells you slugs for vending
      machines and a home remedy.
The entrance fee may or may not be tax deductible.
      The gallery guide is written
in fake Braille and extravagant Latin.
      The ticket stubs are poison ivy
so hold on tight.

ANNUAL MIGRATION OF MELANCHOLY BIRDS

We used to watch the late, late news
       before they played the frayed tape
of the waving flag for the national anthem
       sign-off to test-pattern blues.

Do stations still go off the air? Is some
       poor soul still selling Ginsu knives
and Veg-O-Matics? I sign off early these days.
       The day's first birds are mine now—

we used to pass them at the time clock
       after the late-late-late news—
the anchors either joked around or took
       themselves too seriously. Remember?

I get news 24 hours a day now. If you were
       with me still, would we turn in early
together? Would we buy the hits
       of the 60s, 70s, and half the 80s?

March here, birds returning from wherever
       they go. The ones who stayed
are sneering—or so I imagine.
       I don't think birds imagine much.

       I wish I had more instinct
like in the night-owl days before you played
       yourself off, idling in a garage
with your favorite mix-tape, exhaust

forever ending your exhaustion.
       The spring birds trill shrill,
maybe trying too hard. I have stopped
       falling in love with singers on the radio.

A new pill bottle rattles in my ratty old vest—
       blue eggs in their nest. The news?
As grim as ever, regardless of tone or attire.
I say this on the authority of no one.

God bless America.
       I will not speak of hatching.

FILL OUT SURVEY FOR YOUR CHANCE TO WIN

If you're at home watching a movie
on your movie-watching device of choice

and somebody calls you up
to say they've got some bad news

and you press *pause*
as the train pulls out of its dreamy station

and they tell you someone you love has died,
do you ever watch that movie again?

And if so, what happens when you reach
the part where you paused?

Or maybe you should just pick up
from that moment? Or should you

just leave it there, freezing the train
forever in that terrifying green valley?

THE SLEEP MACHINE COMETH

This white noise generator creates a calming sound environment, making it easier to concentrate, relax, or get some serious sleep, producing the soothing "shushhh" of rushing air…an adjustable housing surrounding a two-speed electric motor…recommended for infants, restless sleepers, shift workers, students, spouses of snorers, apartment dwellers, many others.

It sits on the floor or inside your head,
a giant eraser or an imaginary sea—
sea without salt, a cleansing sea.

The sleep machine has two speeds,
sleep and death. The sleep machine
hushes whispers. Or amplifies them.

You know—*those* whispers.
The sleep machine adjusts the rhythm
of your heart. The sleep machine

takes no prisoners. It is a prisoner.
Or prison. The sleep machine smothers
worries. Or else, leaves that to the pills.

The pills concentrate their sleep serum.
No room for the truth in that borderless land.
The cost is the loss of dreams. Dreams

are pets you've put down. Mercy
has nothing to do with it. The machine
adjusts from *break your neck* to *overdose*.

It does not include the voice
of your mother saying *there, there, just
a bad dream*. Instructions are written

in invisible ink to be read while asleep:
What? *What?* The sleep machine resigns you
to deafness. Or thrills you with it. No one

creaking in the halls tonight. No one dying
hundreds of miles away. No one telling you
what they really think. The sleep machine

unwinds into a measuring tape that spells
your secret name. You save your old sleep
machine just to look at. Sometimes, that's

enough. Nothing's ever enough. The machine
doesn't speak to the alarm clock. The pills
are envoys. Jesus knocks softly on your door.

You know what he wants. Adjust
the machine to the serpent's hiss. Adjust
it to the highest setting: melt your soul.

SHROUD OF TURIN

It is the single most studied artifact in human history. Since arriving in Turin in 1578, the shroud has only been displayed a few times each century.

My brother on business in Milan took a train
to see it. He told our blind mother it renewed
his faith to see what she does not need to,
reading the Braille of her beads each night.

Prostate cancer, like our father. No scientific
dispute. He recites a numb prayer of numbers.
I, who have no faith, buy us a round of it.
Science and religion both play for keeps

despite different scoring methods.
They study the hell out of it for proof
of heaven. If seeing is believing
then I believe in everything I've seen.

Prostate. *Prostrate.* In worship or humility.
If we have souls, who will conduct
their biopsies? Will we have autopsies
instead? Can we ever find anything

unless we throw off our shrouds
and rise to look over the shoulder
of those with science on their side
and stand there—wherever—and say

hmmmm? And make a judgment call
based on the faith of geography
and the grief of mathematics.
My brother's voice elides into a slight

trembling sigh. He stood in an endless line
to see it. If we had a map of the soul
I would be crumbling it into a ball.
I hang on to his voice over the phone.

Like our mother with her beads, I cannot
see him over there, studying for the miracle.

TOUGH GUYS ON FACEBOOK

There they are: Marco Meathook, Fat Freddy, Mean Gin-o,
Two of the three Bruise Brothers. What are they up to now,
fat and tattooed, gaunt and tattooed, still buff, tattooed?

Smiling shy or with mug-shot bravado, cradling
grandchildren, arms around kids legit and illegit,
and bewildered/loving spouses/hook-ups/exes,

or alone, hunched over the fire of a beer or Starbucks.
They stare back at me baldly, but I remember
their long stringy hair of spit and slurs, rattling

me against a wall of lockers for change, for drugs,
or just because, shoving me into the trash beneath
bleachers, behind auto shop, in the Warren Guns

parking lot. Hard. Tough. Greasers. Rockers. Hoods.
At their computers. Got a smoke? Got a light? Impact
of a meaty fist in the gut. Marco could be an usher

in church with that warm, holy grin. Bruise
Brothers? Polite funeral home employees.
Fat Fred? Slimmed down into a gentle sag.

They had jobs, which they kept or lost,
like the rest of us. They had bosses.
They took and continue to take out trash.

Someone loved them once, or twice. Too old
to be anyone's muscle, they muscle their way
onto my computer screen. What do they want?

To be friends.

THE HARDENING OF THE AMERICAN HEART

Jell-O disappeared from the landscape
along with pudding and all soft, sweet things.

Jagged barking dogs lit up the night,
angry at the fact of chains, fences.

Some believed they had God's private number.
They tattooed His face on their chests.

Others did not believe at all, abandoning wrist-
watches and sugar-free gum, cling-free wings.

The reporter reporting on the report plagiarized
His smile and embellished parentheses.

A woman dressed in maps performed weather,
dancing extreme numbers, gleeful with sleek malice.

Enough malice to go around, spread on white bread
like thick peanut butter to stick to the roof

of any mouth considering forgiveness. Repeated
lies layered onto truth like ice hardening opaque.

Except for that one spot. Those who found it
were blamed for warmth, then choked in the noose

of the rescue rope. Those who could afford it
afforded it with tight fists and bloody

abandon. The rest of us, toothless,
nostalgic for the soft, the sweet.

JIMI HENDRIX, NATIONAL ANTHEM

Everybody read all this historic shit into it
when it was just Jimi stoned and messing

around. How many times have you listened
to it the whole way through? Everyone I knew

lifted the tone arm after the first few notes
like *yeah, yeah, we get it, Jimi.* The song sucks

no matter what you do to it, and this crazy notion
I feel at every sporting event is that if I don't take

my hat off somebody's gonna kick my ass
so I take it off and so does everybody else

many of who probably were not wearing hats
back at Woodstock and had more hair then

but it's like we gotta do this now—otherwise
people will think we don't love our country

and all the soldiers who die for it. Though
nobody's whistling it as they work,

if you know what I mean, right, Jimi?
I'd take my hat off for "Wild Thing."

TURNED

Sometimes it's better to toss
the grimace of bad juice, to erase
old scores, or at least smudge them
into dark blobs, to approach the angel
in dark glasses outside the church

and say *hey, got a light?* We say juice
has *turned* as if it could choose
direction. The voice on my machine
wants to know *can we get together just to talk?*
My coffee tastes like soap. Should I call

back? If I counted how often periods
turned into ellipses, I could hip-hop
a bunny trail of dots to any random star
and perhaps back. Or else leave myself
stranded. Maybe it's the fear

of black holes, free fall, or that crick
in the neck after a bad night
in an Econo Lodge with the bass
fishermen on motorcycles.
This is me, she said, knowing
I would know that she would know

that I would know. She sounded
like the world's softest drill
though if I play the message backward
she might be hissing *die like a pig.*
Sometimes it's better to take one last

bad sip. Sometimes it's better
to leave the period there.
Tonight I circle and enlarge it
into a target and shoot tiny arrows
and call every shot a bull's eye.

FILLING OUT THE HEALTH EVALUATION QUESTIONNAIRE

I have been troubled. I continue to be troubled.
I have farted and burped and will continue to do so.
I have a history of a loss of consciousness at night.

I self-treat hunger, and snack frequently,
in mockery of the clockery. God was once
my primary care physician, but he no longer

takes my insurance. Angels buzz in my ears,
and I see halos around lights, but I am taking
my vitamins. I am allergic to advice

and helium balloons. I am over my affair
with recreational drugs, though they still
call me late at night to breathe heavily.

My hair thins with vivid dreaming.
I have many occasions per week, but I'd like
more occasions. More opportunities to tremble.

I notice an unusual taste in my mouth
after eating unusual things. I perspire easily
in the face of the halitosis of shallowness.

I prefer day sweats to night sweats.
I've noticed changes in thirst.
I have been in love. It's a chronic condition.

I bruise easily. I have lost the ability to play
the bongos and tolerate oldies stations. My heart
has skipped at the faint voices of my dead.

I have experienced loss of hearing
and sensitivity. There is a history of death
in my family I believe I have inherited.

0° AND WITH WIND CHILL IT FEELS LIKE 0°

Is zero the proper temperature
for a healthy soul? I know nothing about
the soul. I have no statistical soul evidence.

Right now, I feel the soul in my right ear
making this crackling noise
in the language of the soul

but I don't speak soul. I do know
you shouldn't burn the soul.
Imagine the smell. I can't.

Maybe that's good. I shave
my soul patch. I do not believe
my soul wants a patch.

I look out the window at zero degrees
this morning. I almost wrote *this summer*.
That would be a soul thing to write.

Steam rises from the dryer vent
exploding into memory: as a child
I played for hours in fresh snowfall.

I took off wet mittens or gloves
and placed my red hands under
the vent spewing warmth like—

the soul's volcano? I was cold
and warm in that tiny ball of happiness.
Come in and get out of those wet clothes,

someone may have shouted
from a door cracked open
or through a clouded window,

but the soul, O, the soul
was not listening.

SMELLING THE GRIEF

The weight of dead bodies can tilt
the earth. We are too tired to notice.

Or maybe asleep. Or I am all wrong
and the trees have legs and the weeds

have headphones tuned to Mother Earth
and our feet are constantly abuzz.

On the other hand, one scientist collapsed
from exhaustion after years of calculating

the weight of one grief. His handkerchief
was blue, and large black birds were not

unhappy. I lost my job covering nuance
for local TV news. They said I mumbled.

Ah, light the exploding cigars, mates,
and electrify the white house

and write down your thoughts
and—I meant white mouse—and electrocute—

Electro-Cute—I'm going to copyright
that, and bring out a line of something.

Hey, did you just feel a little tilt,
one shoulder dipping, one leg staggered?

No? You know how light summer rains
can let you smell them rising back up?

Like today. A little sun, so I go out
to look for a rainbow, but all I smell

is grief. I stand on the sidewalk
looking around for someone to ask,

Can you smell it too?

WE SHOULD ALL TOUCH OURSELVES

every so often, regardless
of current attachments or linkages
of appendages, to keep the meaning
of *in touch* pure, even just for ourselves.

I'd like to touch a lot more people—
stroke the hair, curl it around the ear,
caress the shoulder, the cheek,
and obvious places lower on the spectrum,

the horizon, below the limbo line, but I mean,
the human magnet—did someone reduce
its power, turn it off completely?
Has the lack of trust busted

the penny arcade of human connection?
Who will tell my fortune now?
Who will soft-shoe in a clown costume
and sing me some old hoedown classic?

The sting of the stare at the hand
on the shoulder—I meant no harm—
we're both human beans and the sun's
shining, but the humidity is low

and the air crackles like a fall apple
with humanimalness. Can I have
this dance / this dance / and this dance?
Can I touch this part / this part /

and that part? I'll shut up now
and go in a room alone and touch myself.
Yeah, I'm still here. That's all I need
you need to know.

NEVERTHELESS

If it's a contest to see who has the worst
life, none of us with computers

or pianos will win. We line up to tell
our versions—poignant, heroic tales

of woe—hoping someone licks
a gold star, sticks it to our forehead.

Did you eat all of your vegetables?
I ate all of my vegetables. Even

canned peas, even mushy asparagus.
None of us with vegetables would win.

My cousin's girlfriend's grandmother
once met a starving child in Africa.

If the choice is kill yourself
or write a poem. If you kill yourself

to write a poem. If you write a poem
about killing yourself but do not

kill yourself. Then—then—don't kill
yourself, okay? Play a game

on your computer. Cheat so you win.
Count your lucky stars. Me,

I've got a box full of them
ready to be licked, the box

as light as a feather. The feather
that floats above all our grasping.

ABOUT THE AUTHOR

Jim Daniels has published sixteen previous books of poetry
and has won the Milton Kessler Award, the Tillie Olsen
Prize, Blue Lynx Prize, Brittingham Prize, and others. His
fifth book of fiction, *Eight Mile High*, was chosen as a
Michigan Notable Book. A screenwriter and producer, his
films have appeared in numerous film festivals around the
world. His poem "Factory Love" is displayed on the roof of a
racecar, and two of his poems will be making a trip to the
moon as part of the Moon Arts Project. He has been featured
on "Prairie Home Companion," Garrison Keillor's "Writer's
Almanac," in Billy Collins' *Poetry 180* anthologies, and Ted
Kooser's "American Life in Poetry" series. A native of
Detroit, Daniels is the Thomas Stockham Baker University
Professor of English at Carnegie Mellon University in
Pittsburgh.

ACKNOWLEDGMENTS

Ascent: "The Shroud of Turin"; *Briar Cliff Review*: "Nevertheless"; *The Chiron Review*: "0° and with Wind Chill It Feels Like 0°"; *Clementine Poetry Journal*: "Horizontal Hold"; *Confrontation*: "Teaching the Spider to Fly"; *Crab Orchard Review*: "Tough Guys on Facebook," "Filling Out the Health Evaluation Questionnaire"; *Far Out: Poems of the Sixties*: "Jimi Hendrix, National Anthem"; *Ghost Town*: "Taking Painkillers After Surgery"; *Gulf Coast*: "A Brief History of Evolution"; *HeArt*: "Aftershocks" (part one); *Heron Clan Anthology IV*: "The Hardening of the American Heart"; *Kestrel*: "Idiot's Guide to Genius-hood"; *I-70*: "Thimbleberries," "Yelling Fire"; *Louisiana Literature*: "Holy Water"; *The MacGuffin*: "Small Talk"; *The Manchester Review*: "The Middle Ages"; *Michigan Quarterly Review*: "In Case of Emergency"; *Mudlark*: "Middle Ages," "Solstice with Raspberry," "String, January, Schenley Park, Pittsburgh"; *North American Review*: "The Hardening of the American Heart"; *One*: "Aftershocks" (part two); *Parts of the Whole: Poems About the Body*: "We should all touch ourselves"; *The Paterson Literary Review*: "Martin Luther King, Jr. Day"; *Pleiades*: "I want to be in a club named for an animal"; *Plume*: "The Alone-Doors"; *Poet Lore*: "Brushing teeth with my sister after the wake"; *Poetry Northwest*: "After the empty wine bottles"; *poetrymagazine.com*: "On Seeing an Aerial View of the Peace March," "Lighten Up, but Watch Your Head"; *Red Rock Review*: "Smelling the Grief"; *The Same*: "Urban Explorers, Schenley Park," "Safety Lines, Schenley Park"; *Santa Clara Review*: "*I Love Dirty Pussy* graffitied"; *Santa Fe Literary Review*: "Sleep/Balm"; *Slipstream*: "Slight"; *The South Carolina Review*: "Slicing Celery"; *South Florida Poetry Journal*: "Jim Daniels Misses His Ten-Cent Tip as He Prepares for an Unpleasant Meeting"; *Sugar House Review*: "Photo Ops: Where Empathy Begins," "Update on/Elegy for the Here and Now"; *The Southampton Review*: "Good Teeth, Spring Break," "On Our Answering Machine, Bob Plays the Harmonica"; *Spoon River Poetry Review*: "Man with Child, May"; *The Sun*: "Last night I drove my son home," "Heat of Departure"; *Talking River Review*: "Annual Migration of Melancholy Birds"; *Tygerburning*: "Turned"; *Voices de la Luna*: "Growth Chart"; *West Branch*: "Museum of Betrayal"; *The Xavier Review*: "Thrashing"; *The Yale Review*: "Hearing Loss in Late Middle Age"; *Zone 3*: "The Predictable Nature of Tragedy";

Some of these poems also were published in the chapbook, *Apology to the Moon*, BatCat Press.